# Fire

## Words by David Bennett
## Pictures by Rosalinda Kightley

A BANTAM LITTLE ROOSTER BOOK

TORONTO · NEW YORK · LONDON · SYDNEY · AUCKLAND

Fire is very important to us.
Fire keeps us warm. Fire gives us light.
Fire helps us to cook food.

A long, long time ago, people did not know how to make fire. Their light and heat came from the sun. At night and in winter they were cold. The food they ate was not cooked.

Somehow people learned how to use fire.
They may have used a burning branch from
a tree that had been struck by lightning.

Or they may have used burning
rocks from a volcano.

Then people learned how to *make* fire.

No one is sure how it happened.

They may have rubbed sticks together until
they were hot enough to make a spark.

Or they may have hit two rocks together to make sparks.

Today we use matches to light fires. We burn wood in fireplaces or stoves, but we also heat our homes with coal, gas, or oil, which come from under the ground.

Remember, a fire is very hot.

You must never play with matches.

A tiny flame can turn into a raging fire.

A big fire could even destroy a whole
town or forest.

Firemen fight fires with water.
In cities, they connect long hoses
to water pipes called hydrants.

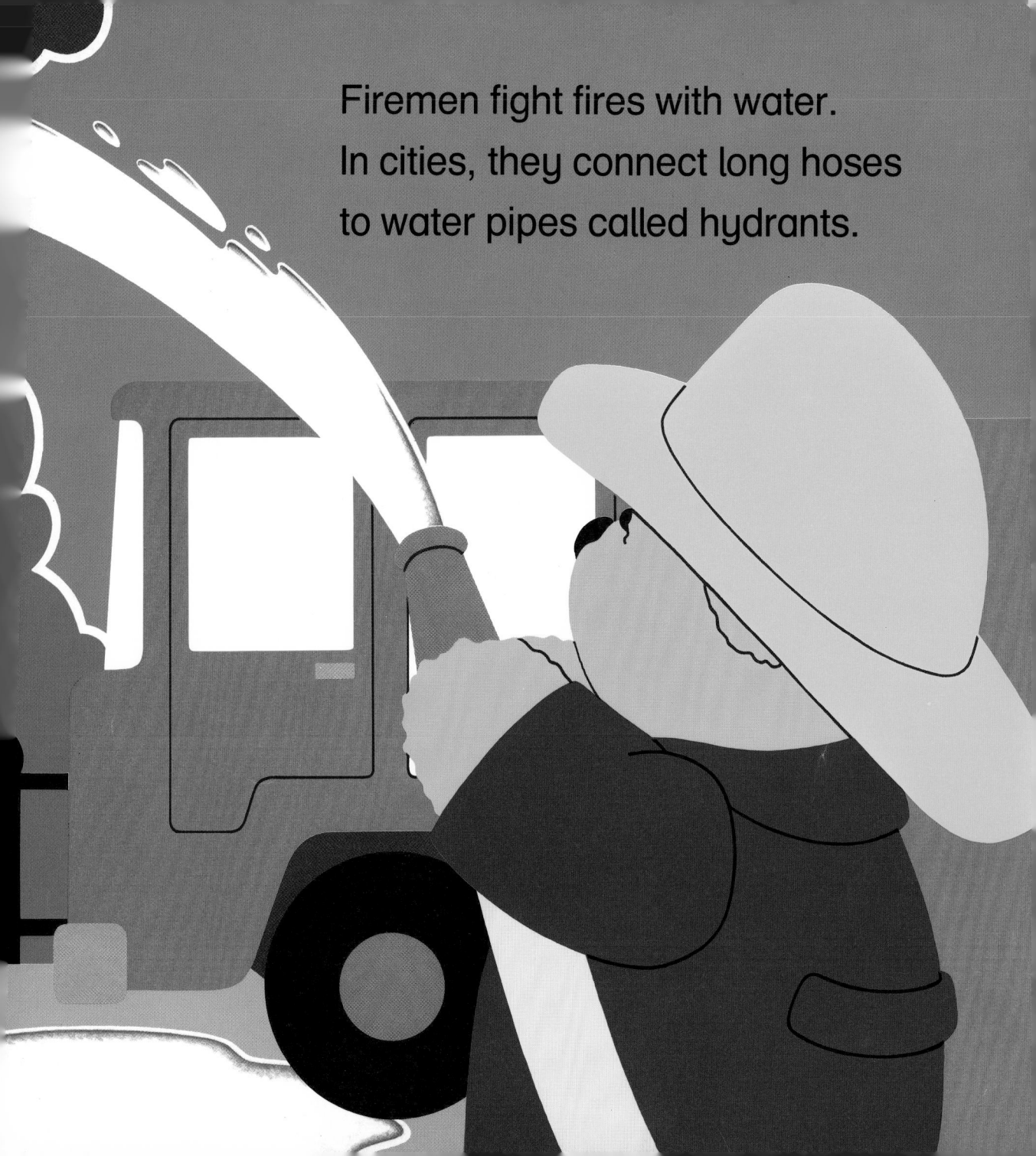

Fire needs air to burn, so sometimes
firemen put out fires by covering
the flames with foam or sand.

Fire makes a lot of smoke, so firemen
wear special masks to help them breathe
and to protect their eyes.

Fire is useful to us in a lot of different ways.
A hot fire can make hard metal soft.
That soft metal can be bent and twisted
into different shapes.

A welder uses fire to join pieces
of metal together.

Fire is used to make some machines work.
Some trains keep fires burning in their engines.

The fire heats up a tank of water.
The water turns to steam, and
the steam pushes the wheels around.

Fire helps send rockets into space.
A rocket engine burns special fuels
to give it the power it needs.

On some holidays we light fireworks.
They light up the sky with beautiful colors.
It is always best to watch
fireworks from a safe distance.

As long as you are careful, fire can be enjoyed.
It makes a birthday cake very special.
Blowing out candles is always great fun.

How many candles do you see?

# BEAR REVIEW

1. We need fire to keep us warm,
   cook our food, and give us light.

2. Fire can be dangerous because it is
   very hot. Never play with matches or
   fire. Never go too close to any fire.

3. We burn wood in our homes.
   We can also burn coal, gas, and oil,
   which come from under the ground.

4. When fire is used properly, it
   helps us run machines, make tools,
   and light fireworks.